ADAM'S DIARY
A REFUGEE'S STORY

Michaela Morgan

Illustrated by **Cathy Brett**

OXFORD
UNIVERSITY PRESS

Letter from the Author

We all like reading diaries. Don't we?

It's a chance to step into someone else's world and share their thoughts, their visions, their feelings. One of the wonderful things about reading books is that we readers get a chance to see the world through others' eyes. And there are so many different sorts of lives. So many different experiences for us to share and understand.

Many of us will never experience exactly what a refugee experiences. This is all the more reason why we should try to understand it.

As a writer I want to tell stories to entertain – and to enlighten. I write to share thoughts, feelings, experiences – and to build connections. That is what I have tried to do with *Adam's Diary*. I wrote this fictional diary in the first person so it 'seems' autobiographical, but it is fiction. However, it is a fiction that represents the true life experiences of many.

I write all sorts of things – fiction, non-fiction, poetry. This 'diary' combines elements of all these types of writing. I hope you enjoy it.

Michaela Morgan

Wednesday 14th September

I DO NOT WANT TO DO THIS. Not at all. But I have been told to. My teacher has given me this book. It's a nice book. It has a red cover. And many blank pages. Many, many, many blank pages.

It's like gazing out at a snowy field. I don't want to make my footprint on it.

She gave me a black pen, a blue pen, a green pen, a pencil, an eraser and a ruler and she said: 'This is your homework for this term. Keep a diary. Write every day. Even if you have nothing to say. Write.'

So I am writing.

And what I am writing is this –

I HAVE NOTHING TO SAY.

Nothing.

NOTHING.

Thursday 15th September

Writing is HARD.

My teacher says I have to practise every day. She says I should write whatever I want and show it to her if I like. She will help me with spellings and things but I must 'feel free' to write what I like and if I don't want to show her, that's OK.

The first thing to work on is my handwriting, which is why I have to WRITE this with pen and paper.

Then my spelling ...

I called this my Dairy at first and Miss Noon laughed. 'Dairy? Are you sure? Check your spelling!' she said. So I crossed out my title ADAM'S DAIRY and rewrote it –

~~ADAM'S DAIRY.~~

ADAM'S DIARY.

I wish I had the latest phone or a cool laptop or a tablet – or my own computer back home – but I just have this red notebook and these pens. And today she has given me some glue to stick things in.

Her name is Miss Noon. She is the first teacher I have had in this country.

I can still remember the teacher I used to have back home in my own country. I sometimes wonder what happened to him. He was tall and strict but he had kind eyes. The last day I saw him, he had worried eyes.

I wonder what happened to him and to the other teachers and to all my school friends. Are they alive, or dead? Are they travelling the way I travelled? Are they still going to school? I suppose I will never know.

I heard that my school was destroyed by bombs. I hope nobody I knew was in the building when it collapsed.

Friday 16th September

This country I am in now is England. It is not my country. It was hard to get here. Very hard.

I am from a place that has more sun and more heat and more colours and more friends and more family ...

... and more bombs, more guns, more explosions ... more dying.

I hope I never see so much blood ever again.

I might tell you about the day of blood. But not now. Now I do not want to think of it.

Saturday 17th September

This is the weekend.

I am not at school but I am writing anyway. I ~~do not~~ don't have a lot of friends here and I don't know what to do when I am not at school.

I live in these rooms called a flat and I share it with my dad and my older brother, Joram. My mum and my baby sister are not here. They are with my grandmother – I hope.

My dad works hard at finding them. He has meetings and he writes letters. He says we must not give up. We must *never* give up. But it has been a long time since we last saw my mother, my grandmother and my baby sister. My baby sister is probably not actually a *baby* any more. I have forgotten what she looks like. Her name ~~was~~ is Leila.

Today I am going to get some shopping and I am going to try to make a meal. I am not good at either of these things but this is what I have to try to do. My father is always busy with papers, trying to find ways for Mum to join us. My brother, Joram, has made friends and he spends time with them trying to earn money. So my job is to go to the shop, find some food and then to prepare our dinner. I hope it is better than the last one I made.

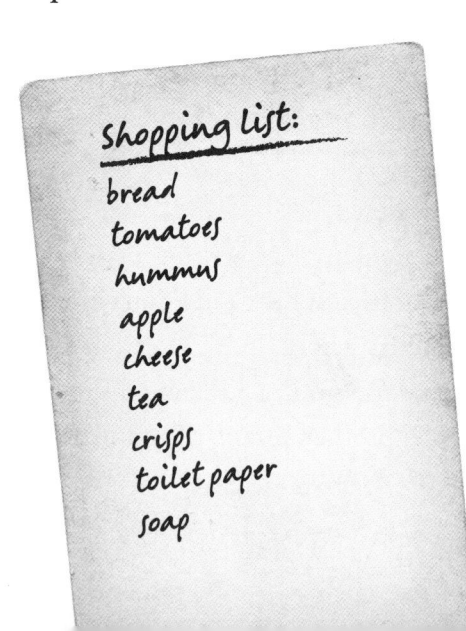

shopping list:
bread
tomatoes
hummus
apple
cheese
tea
crisps
toilet paper
soap

Sunday 18th September

Today I prepare food (a tub of almost out-of-date, bought hummus, a bit of cheap white sliced bread, a tomato that only tastes of water). I eat (not very happily, not very hungrily). I go for a walk (not very far, not very fast).

I watch boys playing football. I wonder if one day I can play football with them. It rains. It is cold. I am cold. I am wet. I go home. I go to bed. That is my Sunday. The end.

Monday 19th September

It is a relief to go back to school. But it is also scary. This school is big. Noisy. There are many boys here – and girls too. We have to wear special clothes – a uniform.

I am all dressed up like a grown-up businessman with a jacket, long trousers, dark shoes, a shirt with long sleeves – and a tie. I don't look like me and I don't feel like me. I feel strange. Uncomfortable. The tie is uncomfortable. Also I do not know the best way of wearing these things. I see that some boys make changes. They wear their tie in a special way. They have different shoes. One wears coloured socks. I stick to the rules. I actually *like* the idea of being invisible.

I think these clothes are to make you invisible.

On Monday we have Maths all morning. I like this subject. It is easier for me than all the subjects that need words. Words and strange letters. Maths is like the maths I did at my old school at home before everything changed. And I am quick at working out figures. I feel peaceful with these figures.

Then it is what they call 'lunchtime'. It is good to be able to get something to eat but it is very noisy and crowded and rushed and quick – and the food is not very good. Not very good at all. I have had so much unpleasant food served carelessly to me in dollops on a tray – here in the jostle of the school hall, or before in the refugee camps.

You queue up with your plate or your tray and – *dollop* – something *almost* warm arrives on your dish. It is something dimly recognizable as food but without the taste or the heat or the care or the time or the sense of home and life you get when eating it. It is food to survive with, not food to relish.

I am glad when I have swallowed the last of it and washed it down with not quite cold water provided in a plastic mug, poured from a plastic jug. You can taste the warm plastic more than the water. And then ...

... FLASHBACK

I am back. By the magic of memory I am back queuing up in a camp. These are called 'memory flashbacks'.[1]

The doctors have discussed them with me.

They seem real but they are memories flashing back into my mind. I can hardly breathe. I feel as if I am back in the camp. Really. I can smell it. I can hear it. And I can feel it.

I am so empty. Empty, empty, empty. Desperate for food, I gobble it up. It does not fill me. I am always always disappointed. It's over too soon. It tastes of institutions and uniforms. I am left feeling even emptier after the hasty meal.

Now it is not just my stomach that is empty. My heart is empty too. I am empty of hope and home. My heart hurts. I am not just shaking with hunger. I am shaking.

---

[1] Flashbacks are sudden strong memories of disturbing incidents from the past. These flashbacks are unpleasant to experience and often produce a sense of panic or dread.

I am glad when the bell rings and I can return to normality and I can sit in a classroom again.

This is the English class with Miss Noon. She had a quick look to see if I was keeping my diary and she saw all these pages and said, 'Good. Carry on.' Then she said, 'Why don't you write a little bit about your country?'

So here:

I come from a big city. It ~~is~~ was modern and rich and beautiful but it is also very ancient. I know something of its history because my father ~~is~~ was a History teacher and he was always telling us about our wonderful history and taking us to see ancient sites.

My father speaks many languages – Arabic but also fluent French and English. After all my travels I also speak some French, plus a few words of Turkish and Greek and I think my English is as good or even better than his now – I understand nearly everything and can read it well. The writing is hard. Very hard. But this diary is helping.

My father talks of our city and our country and when he talks he has tears in his eyes. People stare at him sometimes. A grown man in the street with tears in his eyes?

They do not understand what he has seen.

I have found photographs. Look at these and you too may get tears in your eyes.

main road before

main road after

We saw some of this happen. We saw beautiful buildings become scattered stones. We saw lovely windows become bits of broken glass. And worse ... we saw what happened to people.

Now it seems unreal.

Tuesday 20th September

Games lessons at school today.

I like games. Today we did running and jumping and passing a stick or 'the baton' and we did something called 'hurdling' where you jump over fences. I am good at this.

Some of the other kids are a bit slow. I am slim and I am speedy. I zoom past them.

I learned how to run and hurdle and jump when I was in that camp. They called it the Jungle.

The Jungle was not really a jungle. I imagine a jungle as warm and green – leafy, full of bird sounds and life and beams of sunlight and colour.

This 'jungle' was more like a big grey puddle. It was dirty and cold and wet. We tried to make it homely but our mission was to get out of it. To do this we had to get on a truck that would take us across the Channel to England.

We would wait until they started driving and we would run after them and try to jump aboard. I got a lot of practice at this. We used to try most nights. Most nights we would fail.

And so I learned how to run and jump, how to fall and fail, how to scramble up, how to recover and how to persist.

'Persist' is a new word for me. I persist. I am good at persisting. I do not give up. I try, try and try again. Then I try some more. You can also call it 'perseverance'. Or 'being stubborn'. I tell myself that it was 'being strong'. There are lots of views on this. Some people think it was right. Some people think it was wrong. For us, it was the only way.

Eventually I did get on to one of those trucks. Some young men had got on first. They had longer legs and more determination. One leaned out and caught my arm as I ran towards the truck and then we both caught my father, one arm each, and we pulled and pulled and eventually we got him on board too. That was a struggle, I can tell you. He was fit, my father, but the truck had started to speed up. It was only our desperation, and the help of others who had got aboard, that managed to heave him up. We must have almost pulled his arms out of their sockets – but it was that or leave him and lose him.

And so in these races in the games lesson I am swift of foot and good at leaping and jumping, good at grasping and passing the baton. I can work in a team. And I don't make any fuss if I fall and get injured.

The games teacher talks to me at the end of the lesson. He says: 'You could go far.'

I have already gone far, I think. *I have gone very far indeed.*

I have a calendar. Today is nothing special but yesterday was Respect for the Aged Day in Japan. In this new country of mine there does not seem to be a great respect for the aged. And the old do not seem to have a lot to do. They look bored and vacant and hopeless.

Back home, my grandmother used to live with us and she was always busy and bustling. She was always chatting and singing and sewing and stirring. She did all the ironing. And smoothing out. She did most of the shopping. She looked after us when Dad and Mum were at work. And she did nearly all the cooking. My mouth waters when I think of the food she used to make ...

tabbouleh ... fattoush ... freekah ... hummus ... manoushi bread ... pastries

... ah the pastries ... oozing with sweetness and sunshine.

I have reached a decision.

If I am going to do the cooking, I will learn how to cook *properly*. I will make food like my grandmother made. I will find a cookery book. I will follow the recipes. How difficult can it be?

My grandmother used to hum and sing and smile as she stirred and chopped. Cooking made her happy. It made us happy to eat it. So I will cook like my grandmother. I will try to cook up some happiness and songs and good smells and delicious tastes and memories of good times in the old days.

Wednesday 21st September

My calendar tells me that today is the International Day of Peace. The TV news tells me that more bombs fell on my home town today. My grandmother is still there. So is my little sister. And my mum. I cannot bear to think of this.

Thursday 22nd September

When my dad and I left our home town we were following my brother. He had gone on ahead. Tall and strong and almost a man, Joram had the best chance and his mission was to let us know if we could follow.

He sent us texts:

> have been on buses all week

> walking, walking

> hurt my head – but been treated by a doctor travelling with us

> storm today

> in a camp will stay here for a rest

> very tired

> walking again

> on a boat

> Arrived! Will phone tonight

Then I set off with my dad. Dad thought I was too young to go by myself. I was eight and a half. We were going to get somewhere good, then he would send for my mum, my grandmother and the baby – when he had worked out the journey and found us somewhere safe to settle.

You see, my little sister was often sick. She could not travel at that time. Plus my grandmother was too old for a lot of walking. Dad would find a way and a place for us to be and then send them tickets to join us. Train or bus or boat tickets. Back then we had no idea how hard the journey was. Or how long the journey was. And how much time and spirit it would take. We had no idea of the dangers we would go through. Or the things we would see.

Now when we try to contact my mother and my grandmother, we cannot always get through. We used to be able to phone easily. We could text when we wanted. We used to be able to send things by post. But now post does not always arrive. Phones do not always work. We do not know what has happened.

Nothing is sure any more. We just hope. And pray.

Friday 23rd September

School. I was told off today for 'not concentrating' in History.

I *was* concentrating on history actually. I was thinking about my *own* history and my own country's history. I was wondering whether our history would have a happy ending.

I started to imagine a happy ending when the bombed buildings suddenly got put back together again. In my mind I could see my school rising from the rubble. I could see the dust clearing and clear air replacing it. I could imagine seeing Grandmother holding my baby sister. And there was my mum. There she was, waving. And smiling …

'Daydreaming again, Adam!' said the teacher. 'Focus on history, please. Stop daydreaming!'

Saturday 24th September

The weekend again – I go to the library. I want to find a cookbook. There are many books in the library but there are hardly any cookbooks.

I ask the lady behind the counter and she goes off looking for books for me. She comes back with a small pile. 'You can borrow these,' she says.

One is from my old country.

I feel quite excited.

I fill out all the paperwork and I get my free ticket. Then I go home clutching a cookbook.

On the way home I go into a charity shop and I see the same book. Yes! The very same book. For sale: 15 pence. It is not very clean. It has some pages stuck together by, I hope, tomato sauce. I imagine that someone from my country has had this book.

They have arrived here like me. But they found this book. They cooked from it. Now they don't need it so they have left it at the charity shop for me.

I imagine they now have a big bright flat with new clean shiny books and proper pots and pans and there are cooking smells and they all gather round the table to eat delicious meals. Fragrant rice. Sizzling meat. Fish. Olives, home-baked bread, fruit heaped high. They laugh together and smile and chat. The grandmother pats heads, the mum hugs, the dad smiles, the baby gurgles, the boy eats from a heaped plate. This book tells their story. I buy it.

The rest of the day I study it. I make lists of ingredients.

Now I know what the ingredients are called in English – I can look for them or ask for them. I think I might not have known their names in the first place. I was only a little kid when I left my home. Or maybe I had forgotten them. But now I look at the pictures and the colours and I can almost smell them. I long to get started searching for these ingredients. It will be like a treasure hunt.

So ... I go to an open-air market and I look around. I know what I am looking for now. Peppers, onions, lemons, fresh herbs – I have a list.

The stallholders chat to me. It is not like the supermarket. In the supermarket I move, invisibly and quietly, picking things and hoping they are right. No one notices me in the supermarket. No one speaks to me. The only one who takes an interest is the man who stands at the door checking that I have not stolen anything. But in this market people are friendly, helpful, chatty – and I can get more for my money.

I see a woman who looks as if she comes from my country. She is looking through fruits and vegetables, picking them up, squeezing them, selecting the best.

I try not to stare at her but she makes me think of my mum and my eyes start to fill with tears. I rub them away quickly.

She sees me. She smiles. She hands me a strawberry.

'Try this,' she says. 'Fruit from England.'

It is delicious.

Sunday 25th September

I can never work out what to do on a Sunday. I have done the shopping. I have made a salad to go with the hummus and bread. It was not bad.

I have tidied up the flat. I have made my bed.

I have no school. I hang around in the flat feeling tired and cramped and caged.

In the end, even though it is raining I go out and hang around in the park. No one is playing football. There are no little kids on the swings. The benches are empty. The world is grey and damp and cold. I shiver and go back to the flat again.

This is when it is good to have this diary. I have something to do.

Today I am going to look at some old magazines my dad found.

There is a lot in there about my country. I am going to cut out pictures and some words and I am going to stick them in this book. I have glue. I have my coloured pens.

Here's a view of the world I once knew.

This is the place where my mum and my grandmother and my baby sister are still living. I hope.

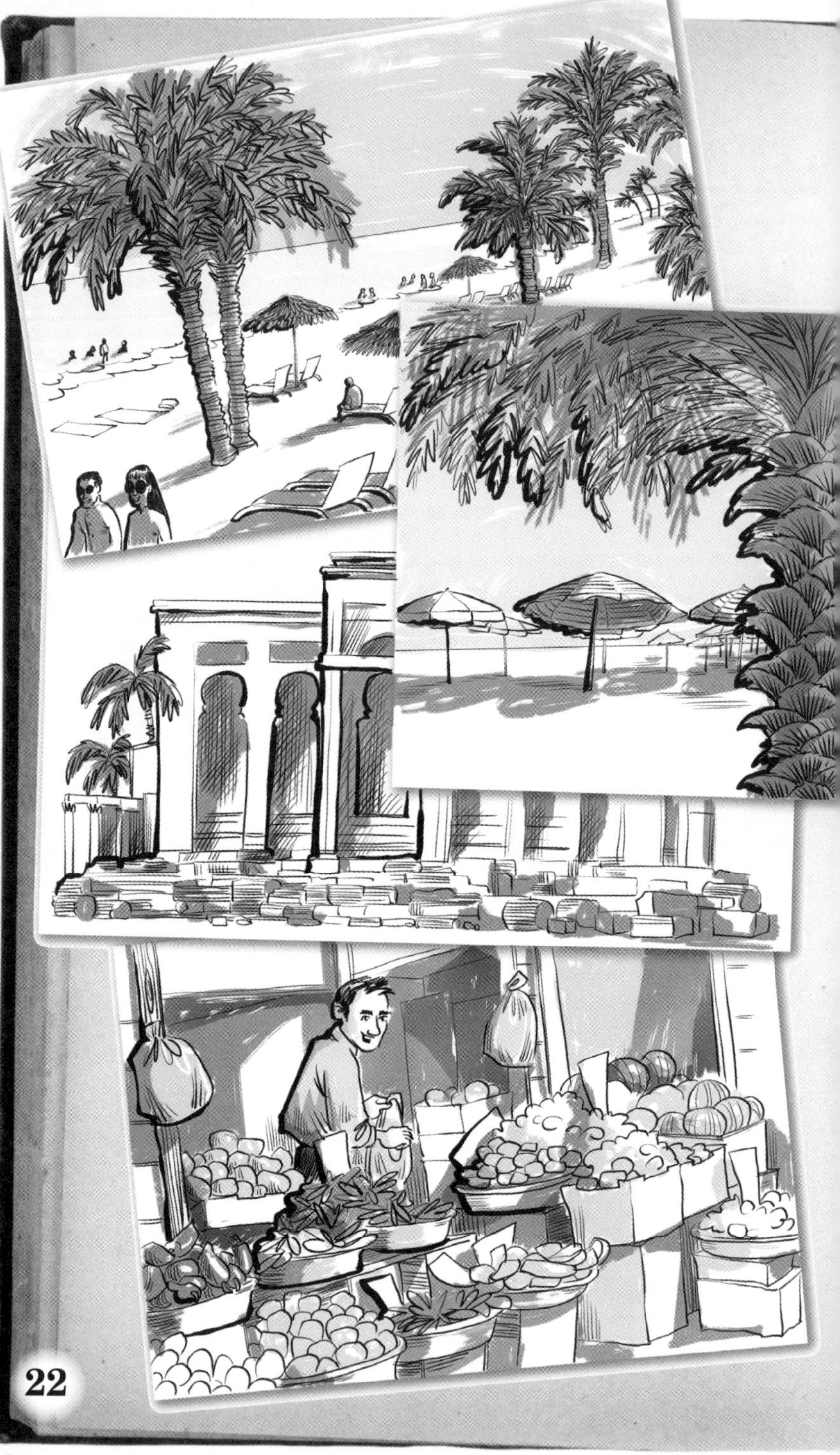

23

Monday 26th September

School today. It was OK. That gang of boys tried to pick on me again. The leader is called Keef I think. They make up names for me and shout at me. I won't tell you what they call me. It isn't nice.

They try to bother me.

I try to ignore them.

Sometimes this is not easy but today I had help.

They were really getting stuck in today. Telling me to go home – as if I could! Telling me I was smelly. Telling me I was rubbish …

And then that games teacher came round the corner and they scattered like crows in a cornfield.

The sports teacher, Mr Jones, was looking for me.

'Adam,' he said, ~~we are were~~ we're having trials for the school team – this Wednesday. You should come and try. You're a good runner. You could do well.'

He shoved a piece of paper in my hands. This is what it said:

Can you run? Jump? Throw?

You could be on our athletics team!
Come for the trials and find out!

Sports field, 1 pm Wednesday and Thursday
Beechfield Academy – be the best!

'Can I count on you to try?' he asked.

Why not? I thought. *Why not? What have I got to lose?*

Keef and his gang often call me a 'loser'. And in some ways they are right.

I have lost a lot of things.

Here's a list.

Things I have lost:
- ☹ My faithful old teddy. I let go of him that very first day. He must be lying in the dust now. Maybe some other kid has found him.
- ☹ That pair of trainers! By the time they went, they were moulded to the shape of my feet. They had become a part of me.
- ☹ My love of swimming.
- ☹ And water.
- ☹ My bedroom with its posters, its books.
- ☹ My collection of football cards, very nearly complete.
- ☹ My whole house.
- ☹ My mother.
- ☹ My baby sister.
- ☹ My grandmother.
- ☹ My heart and hope.

- ☹ My socks with the dinosaurs on them, part of my eighth birthday present from my grandmother. I was wearing them when I left but they were soon worn into holes. Now they are extinct. Like the dinosaurs.
- ☹ My scarf. It smelled of home and kept me warm.
- ☹ My friends. Their voices, their faces, their smiles, their names. I am forgetting so many things about them. They are beginning to fade away.
- ☹ My rucksack that contained everything I loved. Everything I had managed to bring with me from home. That smelled of life and home. That became my teddy to hug. That became my pillow to lie my head on. That floated away into the sea and the darkness.

Tuesday 27th September

When I got home tonight I could hardly see my dad. He was on the floor bent over and had papers heaped all around him. He did not notice I had come in. He was too busy scratching his head and muttering and sorting through papers.

'Money,' I heard him mutter. 'I need to get some money and then – ' Then he saw me. He rubbed his eyes as if he was waking from a dream.

'Sorry, Adam,' he said. 'I'm working out ways we can try to get your mum and grandmother and Leila over here. This paperwork is impossible and we really need some money ... much more money ... '

We used to have money. We had as much money as we needed – so we never thought of money.

Now we think about it all the time.

When we lived in our old country, Dad went off to work to teach history. I went to school. I was good at school. I had lots of friends, good friends. Mum and Grandmother looked after Leila and the house and the cooking and Mum also taught part-time in a college. She was a professor. We had a big house. We had a garden. We had a car. We had lovely food and ... well ... we had everything.

And then we had nothing.

Just like that.

Did you know that one day everything can be fine and normal? And then the next day, *boom*, it all disappears.

And you did nothing wrong. You did nothing different.

You did nothing to deserve it.

Imagine that. You have a house, a family, a room, your own television. Your favourite games. Clothes. Music. A home. A family. Friends. A future.

You are not interested in politics. You have no interest in war. Unless it's a computer game. And then one day –

– CRRRRRRRRRASHHHHHHHH –

It all falls down.

The world comes tumbling down.

Half your house is blown away.

The car is gone.

Your bedroom gone.

The garden becomes a pile of bricks and dust.

Your face is suddenly white – white with the dust from your exploded house.

Your mother is screaming.

Your baby sister is crying. Your dad is running around.

You and your big brother are staring at each other. What has happened? What? How? Why?

And then the days change.

Suddenly you cannot just go to the tap and get water. There is no tap. There is no water. Electricity comes and goes. Your clothes get dirtier and dustier. You do not look like yourself any more.

You are not allowed to flush the toilet. Your computer will not work properly. The TV when it works at all has developed strange lines and squawks.

Most of your clothes are buried in rubble.

But still you go to school.

And there are your friends.

Some of them are just as before but others have a startled look to them. They find it difficult to concentrate. One of them has stopped talking. He just shakes.

What a difference one day makes.

Wednesday 28th September

At lunchtime I ate quickly and ran over to the sports field for the trials.

Those who passed the sports trials could be in the school team and do events and competitions and make the school proud – and I don't know ... all sorts of things. I stopped listening. I just thought I'd have a go because I had been asked to.

Mr Jones, the teacher who invited me, told me to 'give it my best' and then we were off running. Me and a group of other kids. I hardly saw the others, I was so far ahead.

Then there was the hurdling – which is basically jumping with another name. Or leaping. Leaping over fences while running forward. I can do that. I am light. I am quick. I can jump high.

At the end of the trial it was clear that I was good. Better than the rest. I was chosen to be part of the team. There were other kids there who I had seen around the school but I hadn't got to know them. Now I was one of them. Now they were my team. They were my 'friends'.

At last I had friends again.

Which was useful. Because soon I was back in the school buildings and Keef and those boys saw me again and started shouting insults.

'Smelly Adam!' they said. 'Go home,' they started – and then my team came in after me. And we were a group. A big group of friends and that gang of boys suddenly looked small and silly. They split up and went away.

Things were getting better.

Thursday 29th September

My dad was really pleased to hear I was part of the school team. I had forgotten how he looks when he smiles. He looked younger. His face relaxed. He beamed at me.

Joram was pleased too. And jealous.

He had been good at school too. But now he does lots of odd jobs to get money and fills in forms to go to college and waits and waits. His face has set into a sort of scowl. People in the street avoid looking at him. He looks so much older now and angry. He has grown very big very quickly.

'Good for you,' he said when he heard I was on the team but I knew he was also sad because he has no chances at the moment. Now he does odd jobs and washes cars.

Friday 30th September

After school it's running practice for the team.

There I am – me and my new friends.

They went to a cafe afterwards but I didn't go. I do not have spare money for fizzy drinks and cakes and chocolate.

And I have just been told I need to get running shoes. How expensive are they?

Saturday 1st October

I haven't told my dad that I need these shoes. He has enough to worry about.

Instead I went to the charity shop and had a look there.
Nothing suitable.
I don't know what I am going to do about this.
Maybe I will have to leave the team.

Sunday 2nd October

Today I have a plan to fill the day.
I am going to make ...

> Kufta Kebab and a special salad
> and rice with fresh parsley

I go out to find the last few things I need. Then I am chopping and mixing and stirring and tasting.

Dad comes into the kitchen and sniffs the air. He smiles. Then my brother pops in. He grins.

Soon we are sitting down together and eating and talking – and laughing and remembering. I have discovered that food is magic. Cooking is magic.

I am like a magician. I prepare my trick then ...

Hey presto!

the meal arrives and everything is transformed.

I will make the same dish next week or later this week.

I will try to make it better next time. I will add some more lemon, maybe lime ... and coriander or some other fresh herb?

I can spend the next few days looking at recipes, copying them, adding and altering them, replacing unavailable ingredients with those I can get at the market ... copying out recipe after recipe into my notebook – my treasure chest of possibilities, memories, ambitions ...

Monday 3rd October

English today and Miss Noon had a look at my book. Hey – a rhyme ... she took a look at my book!

She TOOK a LOOK at my BOOK
and said
So Adam now you can COOK
and ... now I'm STUCK.
No more RHYMES ...
I haven't the TIME.

And basically I haven't the rhymes – but my English is getting pretty good. I wake up thinking in English and where once I had to think hard to find the English word, I now find I have to think hard to find the word in my own language. My head is filled with words and sounds. They jostle together and confuse me.

I like to find rhymes and new words. Maybe I will never be a great rapper. Or a poet. Or a writer. Or a famous sportsman. Or a popular boy at school. Still I can give it a try ... I can give anything a try. I feel stronger today. Success at sports! A member of a team! A meal cooked and enjoyed – and this diary. Things are getting better.

Tuesday 4th October

I have come a long way since I started at this school. Some of the teachers and some of the other kids have been really helpful and kind. Some haven't. Keef and his mates decided to hate me straight away. I hadn't even said hello before they started.

I don't know why.

But I do know that I have come across worse people and worse situations than Keef. I have survived things he can only dream of. Well, 'dream' is not the right word. The right word is 'nightmares'.

I have got through nightmares. So it is odd that small things (like Keef) can still get to me. I still worry.

At the moment I make sure I stay out of Keef's way and I worry about ending up in a space with just me and his mates because I know what they want to do to me. Their fists are itching to thump me. Their feet are twitching to kick me.

All they can do for the moment is stand too close, stare too hard. They push into me when they are passing in the corridors. They knock into me when I am carrying my tray of lunch. They try to trip me up and barge into me. But I keep on going. I don't even look at them.

But I do worry.

I worry about getting my running shoes and my running kit. How am I meant to find that sort of money?

Then I worry: will I be left out of the team because I have no kit?

If I am left out of the team, will I lose my new friends?

If I lose my new friends, Keef and co. will have a lot more chance to get at me.

So many worries.

Wednesday 5th October

Keef had a go at me again today. In class. We are all reading a book. It's called *Night Flight* by Michaela Morgan and we are given questions and things to discuss. The boy in the book is a refugee. So one of the questions was:

What is a refugee?

We started to give our answers. Keef butted in and his friends joined in. They smiled and laughed as if it was jokes they were shouting out and I was supposed to laugh at them:

A refugee is ...
a stupid scrounger
a lazy layabout
a loser
someone who ...
lives on benefits
wears rubbish clothes
knows nothing

Miss Noon put a stop to their comments but some of the things they shouted out still lurk in my mind like the monster you fear might be under the bed.

Some of their words linger in my ears or stay in my mouth like a bitter taste.

Thursday 6th October

'Today we're going to look at some Shakespeare,' said Miss Noon.

Well ... I was partly intrigued (get my language now!) and partly anxious (you see!) because I have heard so much about Shakespeare. The major English poet and writer. Even back home we spoke of him – but I had never *read* any. So I wanted to know about him.

I had also heard he was really hard to understand and I thought maybe I wasn't clever enough to like his stuff but the thing we read (and said) was great.

> Round about the cauldron go,
> In the poisoned entrails throw.
> Toad, that under cold stone
> Days and nights has thirty-one
> Sweltered venom sleeping got,
> Boil thou first in the charmed pot.
> Double, double toil and trouble;
> Fire burn, and cauldron bubble.
> Fillet of a fenny snake,
> In the cauldron boil and bake.
> Eye of newt and toe of frog,
> Wool of bat and tongue of dog,
> Adder's fork and blind-worm's sting,
> Lizard's leg and owlet's wing,
> For a charm of powerful trouble,
> Like a hell-broth boil and bubble.

We said it together, then we looked at other spells and recipes. I particularly liked the recipes. I am getting to be an expert on them.

A double lesson can seem long but Miss Noon said, 'Now I want you to write your own spell – or recipe. You can work in pairs or by yourself, and your instructions can be to make anything. What magic do you want to make?'

'A spell to make a best friend!' said Daisy.

'To help you score goals,' shouted Will.

'To make you mighty and all-powerful!' said Keef.

'To save the planet from global warming,' said Evie.

I had no ideas and I was working by myself so I spent some time looking out of the window.

I would do a recipe, I decided. I had read a lot of recipes and I knew the language they used – 'Heat', 'Add', 'Stir'.

But what would I make with my recipe? Everybody was busy. Keef was muttering and his mate was writing it down.

I sat alone. My mind wandered.

Keef thought he was better than me somehow. Different. He had no real idea of my life. What would *he* be like if he had seen some of the things I've seen? What would he be like if he'd been through the things I've been through? Some of those things might have worked a spell on him – might have made him stronger, more powerful ... human. Or they might have destroyed him.

Now I knew what I was going to write.

I wrote the recipe title.

Recipe for a Refugee

I started with notes – words, ideas ...

blend in
stir
add
roll
sprinkle
heat
cool
chill
allow to settle
reduce
agitate
whisk
eat
discard

Then I thought of some lines. I thought of the recipes I have read and I was off and scribbling.

Recipe for a Refugee

Take one ordinary child. (Any age will do.)

It could be a boy or a girl.

Separate from friends, from family and from country.

Put to one side. Allow to ...

... ~~Blend in~~

... ~~Settle~~   ~~Add Anxiety~~

... HARDEN

Sprinkle in some worry, stir in some fear. Allow to settle then
ADD AN EXPLOSION.

Crumble homes and heap together

Sprinkle with your most loved possessions, *(the lucky socks)*

Cut away that teddy, those photos, those favourite T-shirts, the lucky socks.

and dirt dust

Toss in tears,
Salt water, salt tears

Divide family.

~~Leave~~ Leave some to rot.

Take away others and drag through dust

For miles and miles.

Thousands of miles.

This is where you add the water.

A lot of water. So much water.

Water as far as the eye can see, and deeper than you can imagine.

Cram child into small boat. Surround with others.

Hold breath. Drench

More salt

> TEARS
> WATER
> SEA
> SEE
> OCEAN

~~Thoroughly whisk? Beat~~

41

At the end of the session I was not finished. My mind was buzzing. We were supposed to hand our work in, but I crumpled mine up in the palm of my hand, held it tightly and took it home. I took it home with me. I compared it to my recipe book.

All that night my mind was full of memories.
I slept deeply. I dreamed deeply. I got up early and I added to my poem.
Then I made a good copy of it. It was legible now. It was clean – not so frenzied and scribbly. I took some things out. Some things sting too much to share so easily. I sharpened and shortened it until it was less rambling, more structured – it was more like a poem.
I looked at my photos. I added some ideas and some words. I took some away.
In the end I had something I was pleased with.

Friday 7th October

I handed my poem in to Miss Noon.
I felt shaky handing it in. I felt exposed. Like a shy sea creature – crawling out of its shell, exposed and able to be wounded. It made me feel raw, vulnerable. But I wanted her to see it – I wanted someone to know who I was.

What I had seen. What I had been.

I wanted them to understand what it was like to be me – what it is like to be a refugee.

After school it was sports with Mr Jones again. It was going well. I learned a few tricks. I know about the best way of starting. No one had to tell *me* to start running at the sound of a gun.

I now know some ways to maintain speed. But it was clear a lot of it was just natural to me. That's what Mr Jones said.

'I think you're a natural,' he said. 'Or have you had some previous training?'

If only he knew the nights I had run for my life. Literally running for my life.

Some of the other kids from the team were going home together. 'We're going to George's house,' they said. 'Do you want to come?'

I hesitated. I had to go home and prepare a meal for my father and my brother but I did not want to say this.

They saw my hesitation. 'Ask your dad and come next time – you can eat and play video games. It's good. You can be one of the group.'

What about that?

I mentioned it to my dad as soon as I got home. And he said yes!

I can go!

That night I found it difficult to fall asleep. I had the impression that horizons were extending in front of me, but this time I was not afraid. I had choices. There would be good times. There would be friends. It would be like a normal life.

Saturday 8th and Sunday 9th October

Have been too busy to write much.

On Saturday I went to the market. I had done lots of recipe research. After that there was the cooking, the eating, the chatting, the smiling. The hope.

On Sunday I persuaded Joram to come to the park with me. I hoped we could play football but there was no one playing (and we didn't have a ball). So we raced each other. He's a better runner than I am. He has stamina – he can keep going much longer than I can. His face grew flushed. His eyes were bright. He stopped looking so grey and so angry.

We were both exhilarated and exhausted at the same time. Went back home. More good food and then I found the time to keep my diary. Here I am now, all up to date. Just have time to get my uniform and homework organized for tomorrow.

Monday 10th October

A normal day.

I can't tell you how happy I am to write that: 'A normal day'.

Tuesday 11th October

My dad was up early. Brushing his suit (a charity shop find), ironing his shirt, shining his shoes, combing his hair. He looked very businesslike. He was off for a day of meetings.

He has complicated plans for getting my mum, my sister and my grandmother over here. The plans seem to involve a lot of paperwork and phone calls and meetings and time and worry.

Today he has an important meeting.

'Wish me luck!' he says. And he's out of the door. It's still very early in the day.

I do a bit of organizing around the flat and then I set off for school.

Maths, English, Science, History ... They all crept by. My mind, my heart, my hopes were all with my dad and his day. I hoped so hard that it hurt my heart.

Time after time I was told off by teachers. 'Focus, Adam!' they said. 'Concentrate! Stop looking out of the window!'

I couldn't wait to get home.

But as soon as I opened the door, I knew it had not gone smoothly. Dad looked tired and crumpled. Worn out. He didn't want to talk about it.

Wednesday 12th October

Miss Noon gave our poems back. She looked at me. 'I made a photocopy of yours,' she said. 'Do you mind? I wanted to keep reading it. It's very good. I thought I'd put it on the wall display if that's OK with you?'

I said it was fine.

'I didn't realize you liked poetry,' she said. 'You might like this book.' She took a book from the shelf behind her desk. 'You can borrow that,' she said. 'Have a read.'

I discover I do like poetry.

I like this one.

INVICTUS by William Ernest Henley

Out of the night that covers me,
Black as the Pit from pole to pole,
I thank whatever gods may be
For my unconquerable soul.

In the fell clutch of circumstance
I have not winced nor cried aloud.
Under the bludgeonings of chance
My head is bloody, but unbowed.

Beyond this place of wrath and tears
Looms but the Horror of the shade,
And yet the menace of the years
Finds, and shall find, me unafraid.

It matters not how strait the gate,
How charged with punishments the scroll.
I am the master of my fate:
I am the captain of my soul.

    I will copy it out. I will give it to my dad to give him heart and strength.
    Because we must not give up.

Thursday 13th October

To give my father extra strength, I made him an extra delicious and nourishing meal.

> Slow-cooked Lamb with green beans and rice

This is lamb steeped in tomatoes and garlic.

I heaped his plate high with the meaty treat. I added fluffy rice.

He ate it all and then wiped his plate with his bread.

'It tastes of home,' he said.

It did.

It tasted of home and love and time and family and care and history and strength.

Joram asked for more. We cleaned the pan with our bread.

'You've got a real talent, little bro,' he said and he smiled. He looked like my brother again. He hugged me. And my dad hugged me.

'I will make it again,' I promised. 'Very soon.'

Then I had a thought. 'And one day I will make it for Mum and Grandmother. Won't they be surprised!'

We all smiled at that.

Friday 14th October

Friday 13th is supposed to be unlucky – but it looks as if I have just missed it! Am I starting to be lucky?

The weekend

Shopping for ingredients, trying things out. Being rewarded with smiles. Then a walk to the park and I spot a couple of my teammates playing football. They wave to me.
And I join in.

Monday to Sunday

I lose track of the days. I am in a frenzy of thinking, planning, selecting, stirring, sizzling, sprinkling, cooking. We are all feeling full. Not just full of food. Full of hope, full of memories. Full of home.
I wish I could tell Mum and Grandmother about my success. They never imagined I would be a cook!

Monday 24th October

I've got permission to go to George's house after school today so I have just left hummus and bread and tomatoes for Dad and Joram to eat tonight.

I go down the street with my team. The feeling of being part of a group is wonderful. I pass Keef and his mates and he looks extra surly. Jealous?

At George's house we eat baked beans and fish fingers, then it's up to his room to play games.

He switches on the screen and I see an image of a soldier with a rifle, with grenades. There is background music. There are sounds of background rumblings and planes overhead.

Two of the boys get the controls and the shots start ringing out and suddenly I feel sick. I run to the bathroom. I throw up. I shiver. I shake. It's another ...

... FLASHBACK

I am in the streets of my home town. Men with guns are coming. There are explosions. Shots. They are coming ...

George's mum comes to find me in the bathroom. I am sitting on the floor.

'Not used to fish fingers?' she says. 'Do you want a lift home?'

But I decide to walk. On shaky legs with the sound of gunshots behind me, I wade through my memories and nightmares, back to my flat and a bath and bed.

Maybe video games are not for me. Maybe they just aren't as much fun as they are supposed to be.

Tuesday 25th October

Dad is off to another of his meetings. He has a bag of papers under his arm and his lips are thin and tight.

We wave him off.

I show Miss Noon my diary at school and she smiles.

'Your writing is good now,' she says. 'Your homework is done! You can stop whenever you like.'

But I like keeping this diary now. I decide I will carry on. Not for school. Not for Miss Noon. Not to develop my English writing – but just for me.

And one day when I see my mum again and she asks, 'What have you been doing all this time?' I can hand it over to her and we can share our thoughts and our memories and we will no longer be separated.

Dad has re-established phone contact with Mum and Gran. They have had video chats.

Mum is OK.

She is well. She is alive.

Gran and Leila are OK.

The house however is now completely gone – which is why post can't get to her. And her bag with her phone was in the house. So was everything else.

She is living in some sort of shelter and has a new phone. My sister has a very bad cough (probably the dust, my mum thinks, but there was some gas and many children now cough a lot). She still needs a lot of medicines and it is harder to get them.

'Why?' we ask.

'Because the shops, the pharmacy, parts of the hospital were all bombed too,' she tells us.

'They're bombing the hospital!' Dad gasps.

'Everything, anything – ' my mum sighs. 'They shell anything ... We live in rubble.'

In the background my grandmother nods.

'We live in rubble,' she says.

'You've got to get out,' says Dad. 'And I have an idea! I know Uncle Waheed is not perfect but he could come with you. We will have to find enough money to pay for him too. You need help with the baby and Grandmother and he has strong arms—'

He stops because Mum has raised a hand.

'He has strong arms,' she says, 'but now he has only one leg. He got shot – he's not in a good way. He's going nowhere ... '

Wednesday 26th – Friday 28th October

I don't seem to have as much spare time for keeping my diary now. So I have a lot to catch up on.

It is so good to be back in touch with Mum. I can see her face.

And I can see my baby sister. Who is not actually a baby now. She waves to me but does not really know what is going on.

In the background I see my grandmother. She is always there in the background but now she does not say much. She looks very tired.

Once when my grandmother briefly left the room, my mum whispered urgently, 'She wants me to leave without her. She cannot make the journey – but I cannot leave my mother here. I don't know what to do – '

Then my grandmother returned and my mum frantically wanted to change the subject. So I helped.

'You'll never guess what I'm doing nowadays,' I said.

'Schoolwork?' she said.

'Swimming?' she suggested.

'I don't swim any more,' I told her. 'I hate it now. Schoolwork is OK. I am doing OK. But what I have discovered is ... I like cooking – '

In the background my grandmother showed a flicker of surprise.

'He does,' my father said. 'He has a recipe book and he invents his own things too.'

'I can't always find all the right ingredients,' I explained.

'He's good,' said Joram. 'He makes some of the dishes Grandmother used to make.'

My grandmother looked less slumped. She was listening.

It seems that my cooking might be feeding her soul too!

Saturday 29th October

My first sports competition as a part of the team!

It turns out that the school *lends* you a running kit. So I have been given shorts and a vest with the school name on. But they do not give you shoes and socks. So I turn up with my school uniform shoes and dark socks on.

I look ridiculous in my heavy shoes and light shorts.

I cannot bear it. So I slip my shoes and socks off and put them in my bag. I am barefoot but my feet are strong and very hard. They are tough as boots. These feet have walked thousands of miles. They could not be any tougher.

A few people glance at me. It looks as if Mr Jones is going to say something but then he holds himself back and we're off and I'm running like the wind, leaping like a gazelle – light and free – my feet pounding the dust and stones as if they were clouds that I am flying over.

I win. By a large margin.

On the way home the chatter is excited. Congratulations are heaped upon me. My back is patted. My photo is taken.

The bare feet are accepted.

It seems they think this is the way we do it in my country. Actually my school was much much better provided for than this UK one I am going to now, but the English seem to think I have spent my life living barefoot in a desert. Possibly with a pet camel.

One day I should tell them all about my country.

How civilized it was.

How beautiful it was.

How normal it once was.

How it all came tumbling down.

How all worlds can come tumbling down.

'Keep alert!' I want to tell them. 'Things happen and you can't do anything about it.'

Sunday 30th October

A mega day of cooking and eating. Salads. Meat. Puddings. Each time I bring a dish to the table, I am aware of the gift I am giving to my family. The life lines I am reconnecting. The love that comes stirred in with the food.

We speak to my mum over a video call and I tell her about our meal. My sister is curled up asleep beside her and my grandmother is slumped in a corner behind.

It looks as if they are all living in the same room in some kind of shelter.

My poor mum – she was so proud of her house and her garden, her artwork, her beautiful clothes, the well-equipped kitchen, the luxurious furnishings.

She seems to be reduced to a mattress and a few bits of clothing. In the background I can see one battered cooking pot.

I remember our kitchen.

My grandmother perks up at the mention of my latest meat dish. 'How did you make that without a tandoor oven?' she asks.

I explain how I had to adapt because I can't always find the right things or afford them and the oven here is odd.

She listens. She nods. She smiles.

She seems to be waking up.

Monday 31st October

They have a special day here in the UK. They call it Hallowe'en. I have tried to make sense of it but I am not sure I have quite got it.

It seems to involve a lot of dressing up as monsters or scary creatures. Sweets are involved. And pumpkins – this is good news for me – I suspect that there will be a lot of leftover and abandoned pumpkins and I can make soup!

It all seems to be something to do with scaring and being scared. I don't really get it.

I have been so very very scared that I would never try to invent ways to scare myself for fun. So I stay well out of it – but I will keep an eye out for leftover pumpkins!

Tuesday 1st November

That Hallowe'en thing is still going. I have gathered

lots of pumpkin-based recipes. It's going to be a feeding frenzy round at our flat.

In my video chat with Mum, Gran popped up in the background to join in with more suggestions for ways of using pumpkins. I am watching her come back to life bit by bit!

When I told her that my friends said that they simply throw their pumpkins away when they have used them for some sort of decoration, she really came to life.

'Terrible! What sort of place is that! Disgraceful! When I was a girl we used to ... ' She is off and she is beginning to sound like a real grandmother again.

I remember the huge meals she used to make. She would heap the table high and we would all be there – family, friends, neighbours, passers-by ...

Hospitality was part of home life.

That night, just as I was falling asleep, I had an idea.

Wednesday 2nd, Thursday 3rd November

Everywhere I went, I asked, 'Do you have plans for your pumpkin – because I could use it ... '

I collected pumpkins, or parts of pumpkins, everywhere I went. I had a small mountain of pumpkins.

After school it was planning and cooking – cooking, cooking – cooking up a storm of pumpkins.

Friday 4th November

I invited everyone who had given me a pumpkin or a part of a pumpkin, plus everyone I know or have ever even met to come and eat at our flat for food and hospitality. Just like my grandmother used to do! It was a party.

We had:
- Soup (my original soup idea with chickpeas and harissa. It's a hearty hot soup.)
- Pumpkin Patties
- Tahini Pumpkin and Stuffed Pumpkin

We served this with a huge pile of salad. We call it Fattoush – it's basically herbs and green things and mint. Lots of mint. I added toasted bread to the salad and everyone heaped their plate.

Our flat was crammed – neighbours, shopkeepers, teachers, friends, their parents, that lady with the cats, the local police officer, the lollipop man …

I took some pictures.

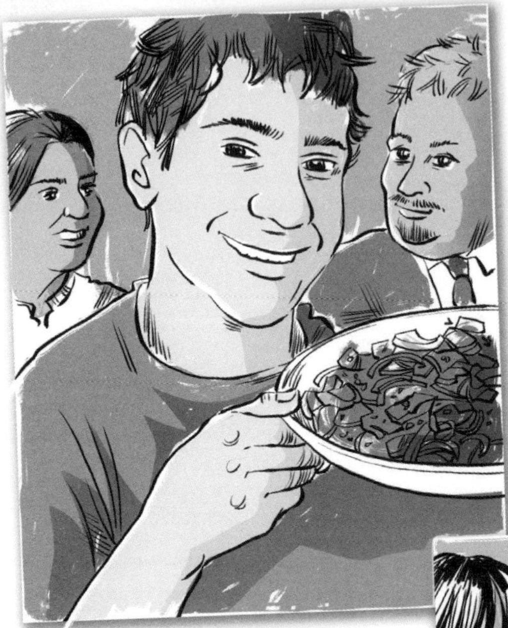

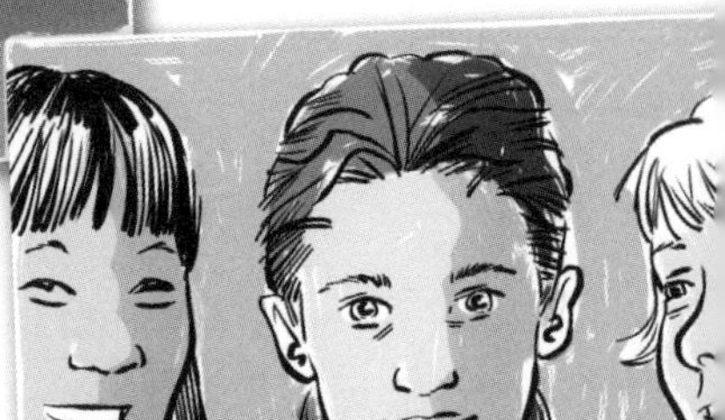

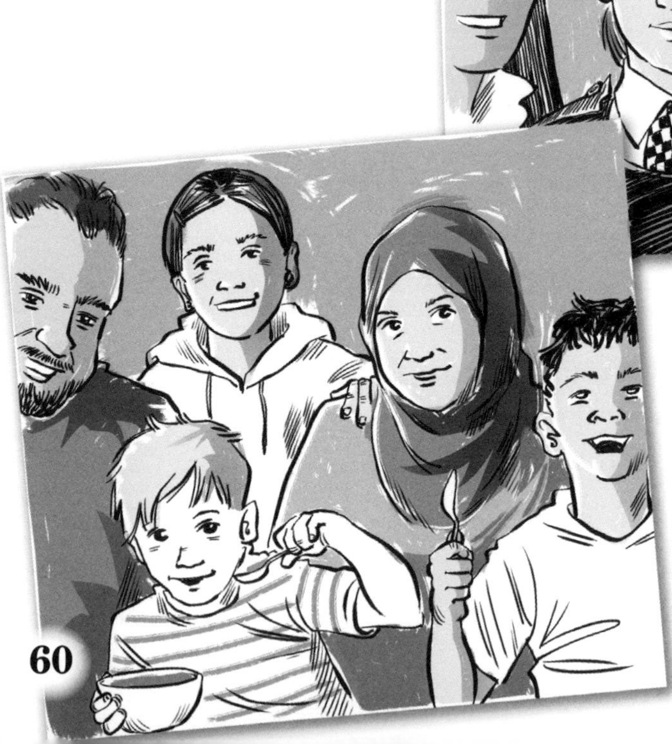

One of the neighbours – the one with the pretty daughter – came back later with a huge handful of mint.

'It grows in my garden,' she said. 'Come and help yourself whenever you want some. It grows like a weed. You could even plant this and grow some yourself.'

Saturday 5th November

Another special day. This one is to do with fire and fireworks. Apparently we celebrate an attempt to blow up the government and then the burning of a man! Strange country! Odd traditions!

But the fireworks were impressive. The colours! The display! I should have loved it. But it left me feeling sick and shaking – too many memories of explosions are in my head.

Sunday 6th November

I saw that neighbour again and she showed me where to find the mint in her garden. Her daughter came out. She has shiny hair and a lovely smile. Her name is Katie.

'I've heard about your cooking and had an idea for you,' Katie said. She shoved a piece of paper into my hand. 'I printed it off the Internet,' she said. 'You should have a go.'

She waved goodbye. 'Food for thought!' she yelled. 'Think about it!'

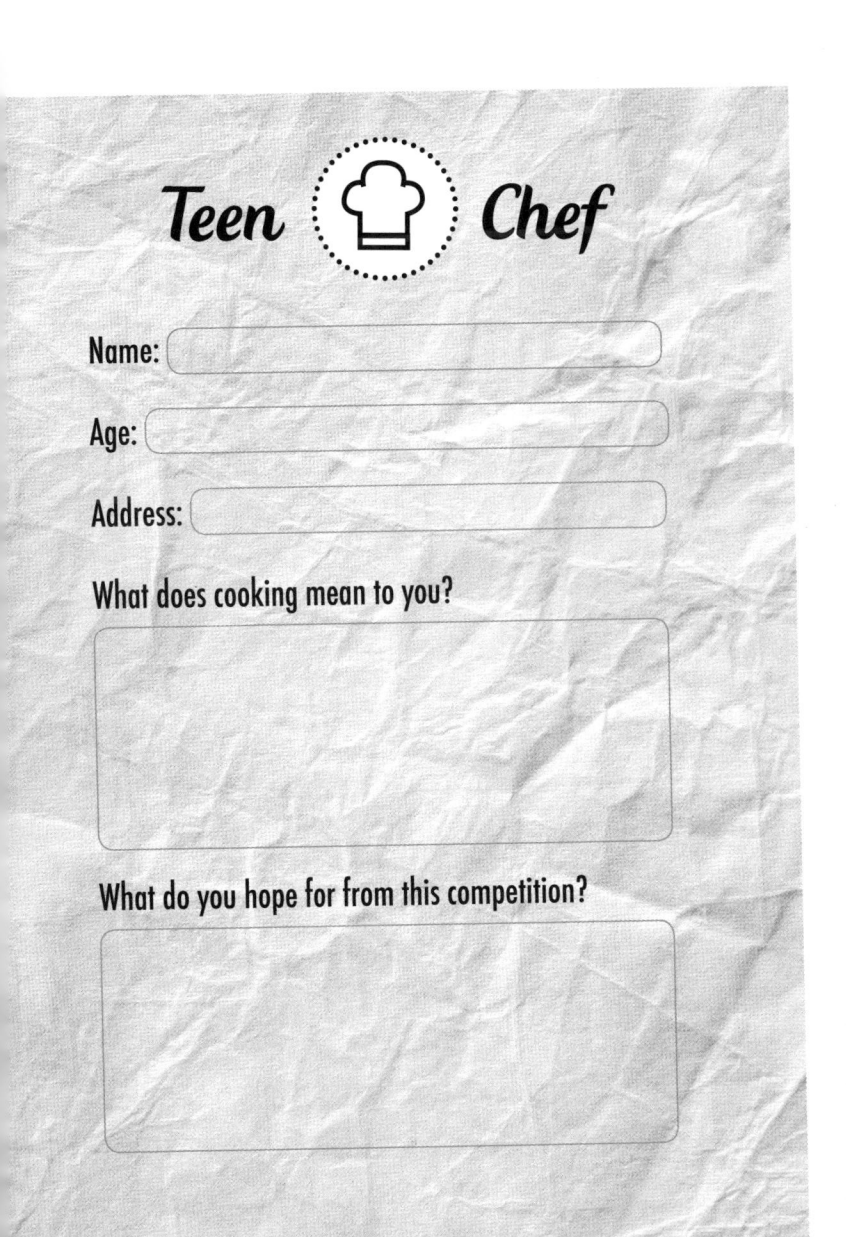

Teen Chef

Name:

Age:

Address:

What does cooking mean to you?

What do you hope for from this competition?

Monday 7th November

I thought about the cookery competition idea all last night.

I thought about it in school today. (History is *still* not getting my attention. How can they make a subject that is so real and so fascinating into something so mega boring? It's quite a talent).

I thought about it as I walked home from school.

I made a meal of all my leftovers from the party.

Then I thought about it some more.

What have I got to lose?

Having nothing much to lose is a great strength, it turns out.

It makes you courageous.

To be part of the *Teen Chef* show ... Hmmm ... I will do it. I will fill in the application form online. I'll do it in the library tomorrow. I could use their computer and their printer and their peace and quiet. I will get that application in.

I would do it for fun.

But there is also the possibility of money.

Yes, money! Thousands of pounds of money.

Money that could help get my mum, gran and sister safely across the seas and to us.

It has to be worth a try.

Tuesday 8th November

I showed Miss Noon my diary and she saw the application form I'd stuck in.

She walked with me to the school library and I saw her chatting to the nice librarian lady.

They set me up in a quiet corner with a computer I could save stuff on, access to the printer and a 'just ask if you need any help'.

I worked on my application until I had to go home.

When I got home I was keen to tell my bro and my dad all about it. But they were yelling at each other.

Joram's face was red, his hair was on end and he was practically screaming.

'You can't do that! You can't. No! No! NO!'

He ran from the room, slamming the door so hard that the flat shook.

My father was shaking too. But he didn't explain to me.

'Leave me alone,' he said. 'I need to think.'

I left the flat and went to look for my brother. He was sitting in a bus shelter.

'Tell me,' I said.

And he did.

Wednesday 9th November

I had a night of nightmares.

My heart was heavy with ... I think it was dread.

I felt stunned. Tearful. Hopeless.

And very very scared.

I dragged myself to school and I heard not a word that was said to me in any lesson.

I was told off in History. Told off in Geography. Even told off in PE.

'Have you got no interest in history?' they asked. Ha! If they only knew.

'Have you no interest in geography?' I must know more geography than they can imagine. I've walked a continent.

'Don't you want to look after your body?' they asked.

If only they knew how very very much I care about those things ...

I headed for the library. It's a good place to hide and I didn't want to see anyone. But Miss Noon was there chatting to the library lady.

'Do you need some help with that application?' Miss Noon asked and she put a friendly hand on my arm.

And I am ashamed to say I burst into tears.

She and the library lady bundled me into a little back office. They made me a cup of tea. They gave me a tissue.

They gave me a biscuit. More tissues. A wastepaper bin.

In the end I had sobbed out my story.

The ladies looked at each other.

'Have I got this right – ?' said the library lady. 'Your father is suggesting that he goes *back* to your home country – to a dangerous war zone. And he wants to leave you and your brother here. Alone?'

'He wants to help get my mum and my sister and my gran out – ' I sobbed. 'He says it's the only way left.'

Miss Noon sighed. 'After all you went through to get here ... after all that – ' She gave me another tissue. And she helped herself to one.

The school bell went for the next lesson.

'I've got to go,' said Miss Noon. 'You're supposed to be in English with me now, aren't you, Adam?'

'Yes,' I sniffed.

She handed me another tissue.

'Well, I give you permission to stay here in the library. I want you to finish that application and get it sent in. Angie will help.'

'Angie?'

'Me,' said the library lady. 'I'll help.'

'You've got a double lesson,' said Miss Noon, 'and I want that application to go off today by lunchtime. That's your project. OK? Get busy.'

I didn't feel much like doing it but that's what I did.

There was the usual stuff.

Teen Chef

Name:

Age:

Address:

But there was this:

> **What does cooking mean to you?**
> **What do you hope for from this competition?**

I really went to town on those.

Plus I scanned pages from my diary – with recipes and pictures of the food I might make, with pictures of my old house, my kitchen, my family, my country, a map, the poem, which I had typed up, and photos of the party with all the neighbours and the friends and the kids and the teachers all squished into our flat eating my food – with big smiles on their faces.

And so the morning passed.

I finished the application. I attached all the scanned documents and photos. Angie helped.

Recipe for a Refugee

Take one ordinary child
Any age will do.
Gather together some well-ripened troubles and
 whisk them up.
Toss them into the mixture.
Sprinkle in some worry.
Stir in some fear. Let it settle.
Heat up until homes begin to crumble.
This is the time to drip in the tears, drop by drop
 until the mixture begins to rise.
Add several shouts and one scream.
Then separate the ingredients.
Add water.
Ensure water is deep, dark, threatening.
A large sea or a small ocean is ideal.
Cram children into a small container. Pack in
 tightly,
Hold breath. Then add salt. Drench thoroughly.
Chill till almost frozen.
Lift out and drain. Transfer to camp.
Leave to stew, slow cook, low temperature.
Shake from time to time then allow to harden.
You have made a refugee.
Now wash your hands.

Angie gave me a celebratory chocolate biscuit. The morning came to an end. The bell went. I left the library. Time to move on.

I am an expert at moving on.

I have moved on from city to countryside, from countryside to desert, from desert to sea, from border to border, from roadside to station, from shelter to camp.

I have moved on from a normal boring lovely life to a life of explosions, disappearances, danger, blood. To an exhaustion I could never have imagined. To an emptiness more deep than I would have thought possible.

I moved on to hunger, from hunger I moved on to drenching and shivering and sinking and near drowning.

From drowning I moved on to drifting in a camp and eventually I got here.

Here. My new home. A little home with my brother and my father, a roof, a bed, a school, a table heaped with food ... and now it was all going to disappear again.

I had to move on.

Thursday 10th November

My application for *Teen Chef* has been sent in. At home all is silent. My father sits with his head bowed in thought. My brother sits in sullen silence.

I am afraid to break this silence and anyway I don't know what to say.

Friday 11th November

nothing

Another week, and another ...

The weeks pass. Too busy to write – sports practice most evenings, training for competitions. Still nothing from the TV company. Miss Noon says these things take time. How can it take so much time? Maybe they just don't want me on the show. I've stopped expecting to hear from them every day, checking for emails ... I'm still cooking, though. Practising, just in case.

Dad and Joram continue in silence.

Saturday 25th February

I need to start writing again today. To try to make sense of what happened at the park.

Joram is in a very bad way. He seems to have lost all energy and hope.

He doesn't talk about it. He just slumps and glowers.

I persuaded him to go out with me and we slouched round the park. He didn't want to go. But he didn't want to stay in the flat with Dad. He is like an unexploded shell. Ready to explode at the slightest thing.

He won't even look at Dad. He hardly speaks to me. He grunts and snarls like an animal.

So it was particularly unfortunate that we met Keef and co. in the park.

They were in a huge group. And, as usual, they were looking for trouble.

This time they got it.

They shouted their usual stuff ...

They crowded round us, jostled us. Taunted and insulted us.

Normally I ignore them. Just walk on. Normally my brother *tells* me to ignore them.

But this time ...

... it was if we'd let a tiger out of a cage.

He turned and he pounced on Keef.

Knocked him to the ground.

Screamed and shouted at him.

Slapped him and punched him.

Went to kick him.

I tried to hold him back but somehow I got involved too. Soon it was a fight between a whole crowd – arms flailing, insults hurling and finally sirens screaming ... and then the drive in the police car to the station where we were questioned and we were given a warning. My dad was called to come and get us. The walk home (or limp home in my case) was shameful. My eye was swollen and half-closed. My lip was cut and bleeding. I was cut, scratched, bruised. My clothes were dusty and ripped. I looked and felt a state.

It might get worse. As we came out of the police station

we heard a click, saw a flash. We had been photographed. We were news.

Sunday 26th February

Miserable day. Rainy cold. Dad furious with us.
Us black and blue and aching.
And worried.
So worried.
With due cause.

It seems we have made it into the newspapers.
And nothing good is being said about us ...
They call us 'troublemakers'. And worse. Much worse.
And they write about Keef as if he is some sort of innocent victim. He will be impossible after this.

And I have to go to school tomorrow and face him.

Monday 27th February

It didn't go well.
Keef had made copies of the newspaper article. He scattered them around the school.

Everywhere I looked I saw pictures of me looking sullen and swollen. Surprised by the camera flash, my mouth is wide open as if I am shouting. I have one eye half-closed and swollen. I have a wild and dusty bashed-up look. I am unsmiling. I look fierce.

Like a monster ...

I missed out on lunch and took refuge in the library.

Angie nodded to me. She tried not to stare at my black eye and cut lip. I look terrible. I sat by the computer and turned it on.

Bing. There was an email for me.

From the TV production company.

From: Sally@teenchef.com

Subject: invitation to screen test

Hi Adam

Thanks for applying to be on Teen Chef. We really enjoyed reading your application and we'd like to meet you and give you a screen test – a practice film to see how you are in front of a camera. Please come on Wednesday 29th ...

I showed it to Angie.

'Screen test!' I said. 'And look at me!'

I pointed to my black and swollen eye, my cut and swollen lip. 'I can't go. I can't go.'

Angie winced. Nodded thoughtfully.

Then she walked away.

I carried on with my day. The time dragged.

Tuesday 28th February

I didn't want to wake up.

I didn't want to get out of bed.

I didn't want to go to school.

But Dad took no excuses.

So here I am in school. But I am in the library again. I can't face the classroom today.

The newspapers are having a field day on me. And the kids who join in with the crowd – they are crawling out of the shadows and having a go too.

Every time I walk down the corridor I hold my breath, look at my feet and just keep on going.

Keef's group has grown. They are everywhere. I am now known as 'the refugee'.

My refuge is the library.

I spent lunchtime there as well.

Miss Noon and Angie came to find me.

'We've had a chat,' said Miss Noon 'and spoken to the head teacher and—'

Angie interrupted. 'And we see that you need an appropriate adult with you at the TV company screen test—'

'So we will come with you.'

'It's tomorrow afternoon straight after school. Get your dad's permission – ask him to sign this – and we'll meet you here at 4.'

'But my face – ' I said, 'but—'

'You've just got to give it a go,' said Miss Noon. 'We can explain the face – and the fight. Remember, get the permission note from your dad.'

Wednesday 29th February

I am setting off for the screen test. I feel weird.

I think I understand that expression about your heart sinking to your boots. I feel weird being with my teacher and the librarian out of school. They call each other by their first names. Miss Noon is called Stephanie. I have never met a Stephanie before. Or Steph. That's what she calls herself. They call themselves Steph and Angie. They seem to be best friends.

I made an effort with my appearance.

I'd dusted my shoes. I'd brushed my jacket. I'd ironed a shirt. I am far from screen-test-perfect. My eye is not so swollen now – but it is still black. I have dark rings round my eyes. My lip is still a bit swollen and you can see the cuts on my face. One of my hands is bandaged.

But it is the best I can do.

Miss Noon says she will explain to the telly people.

Thursday 1st March

They seemed to know all about my face. I think Miss Noon had phoned them.

They were very relaxed, friendly. They called me 'mate'.

They asked me questions and asked me to talk about the pictures I had sent and the recipes I had made. They asked me to tell them about the party I had given last year.

'Where do you find your recipes?' they asked.

I showed them my cookery book with all the pages stuck together. 'This is what I use,' I told them. 'And my gran gives me advice. So does my mum.'

I told them about the video calls.

I told them how my gran had started taking an interest. How she had stopped sitting slumped, staring at her feet, and had started telling me off and giving me tips and asking me to show her the dishes I had made.

They asked me to read part of my application form out loud and they filmed it.

Then they went out of the room and came back.

'How would it be if we set up a video call to your old home?' they asked. 'And you can tell your mum and gran about the competition. Would that be OK with you?' They looked at Miss Noon too. 'OK?'

We agreed. Things hadn't seemed as bad, recently, when we'd called them.

So there was my mum looking out at me from their big screen.

She gave a brave little smile and lifted Leila's hand to make her wave. But Leila was half asleep or ill. She hardly moved.

In the background there was Gran looking old and tired. She looked up when she heard my voice.

She smiled when she heard my news. 'You had better start finding some good strong cooking pots if you get selected to take part in this,' she said. 'They make a difference. Look at what I have to use now.'

She showed the battered old pan.

'We've lost all our pots and dishes,' Mum explained. 'And our kitchen of course.'

'And our house,' Gran added.

Leila woke and started to cry and cough.

'We'll go now,' said Mum. 'Good luck getting into your cookery competition. Let us know if you need our help.'

'And tips,' said Gran. 'I have top tips – plenty of tips!'

The screen crackled and the picture faded.

Then the telly people said thank you. They shook my hand.

They said I could go home and they would let me know.

I felt a bit better for meeting them. I was almost dizzy with relief. We left the office and took the lift down to the ground floor.

Downstairs in the TV building we found a cafe and Miss Noon started to order tea and cakes and stuff when I realized, 'I've left my cookery book in their office!'

'Run back and get it,' said Miss Noon. 'We'll wait here.'

Off I went, back in the lift. The office door was ajar and I slipped in and saw my book straight away. I stuffed it in my bag and quickly turned to leave. Then I heard voices and footsteps approaching ... I froze. It was the team from the programme. They went into an office opposite and left the door open. I didn't know what to do so I just stayed where I was, silent, hardly breathing.

I heard every word they said.

'So what did you think of that, then?' asked Jules, the producer.

'Let's just see the footage of him reading his application again,' said Sally, one of the researchers.

The film started.

I caught glimpses of the film. Saw my own face looking into the camera. My eyes, ringed with black, my face cut, my lip cracked, my hand bandaged. I saw myself reading from the application form:

What does cooking mean to you?

I realize that cooking is not just about food. It's about care. It's about love. And memories. And home. And family. You take the care to find the ingredients. You mix them together as if you are making a spell. You are making magic. There is so much more to cooking than food! There are the smells when you crush a herb or roast some meat, or chop some vegetables – those smells remind you of your mother and her mother and your family and your friends gathered together sharing and smiling. You are nourishing people with your cookery. You are connecting people with your cookery. You are linking generations and cultures. You are building bridges. You are saving souls.

You are planting hope and growing smiles.

The camera zoomed in for a close-up of my eyes. Then I went on to the next question.

What do you hope for from this competition?

If I won I would have some money. I would use the money to get my mother and my grandmother and my sister on to a plane, if that were possible – a comfortable, safe plane. They could sit down all the way. They would not have to carry their own bags and possessions, if they have any possessions left ...

They could fly over here and live with me, my dad and my brother. They could live here in safety with clean fresh water, constant electricity. Out of danger. Our flat is small here but it has a solid roof. It has taps that work and strong walls and heating – and a kitchen with some pots and pans. How my grandmother would smile to see a kitchen! How well my little sister would sleep in the quiet here – no bombs, no falling down ...

How my mother would hug me. How my brother would learn to smile again.

And my father could put down his papers and look up again!

And when my mother and grandmother and sister got here I would greet them with a table heaped with food that made them feel safe and warm and nourished and cared for and at home.

The filmed piece came to an end and the production team sat in silence.

I waited until they were talking again, then I tiptoed away.

Friday 9th March

Still no news from the telly people. It's been a week already.

Sports practice. My team mates were still friendly despite the newspapers.

Back at the flat, Joram's face is less swollen but his eyes still glower. My father is looking up costs of going back home. He is always on the phone or finding documents or writing emails. Now it seems he is considering taking us *all* back with him.

'At least we would all be together – ' he mutters. 'If I can raise the money we can all go back together.'

I don't want to go back there. The thought terrifies me. But how can we leave Mum and Gran and baby Leila all alone without any help?

Dad's face is tight with worry. He has a mad look in his eyes. He is desperate.

Saturday 10th and Sunday 11th March

Neighbours, friends and passers-by who came to my 'party' last year – and have said hello to me since if we've seen each other – have been popping in over the weekend to tell us not to be bothered by the newspapers.

Katie came with some more mint and a big smile. An old man called with some vegetables from his allotment. The lollipop man popped in to say he'd seen the whole incident – that fight – and had told the police our side of the story. 'You were provoked,' he said. 'They started it. I saw it all.'

A neighbour says she's written to the newspaper to complain about their articles and to 'tell them the truth'.

Life doesn't seem quite so bad somehow – as long as I do not look at the piles of printouts with journey prices and details. *Surely* Dad will not try to get us back there now that we have at least some hope. I ask him this question. He does not answer. He avoids looking at me. My brother avoids looking at him. We are all sharing a small home but all in our separate worlds.

I make some spiced minced lamb with yogurt and fresh mint and I make some bread – Joram and my dad sit opposite each other in silence. They break bread and pass it to each other. Tiny steps forward.

And as a treat I've made some baklava. It's crispy, velvety, sticky with honey and crunchy with toasted nuts. My bro and my dad start by nibbling but soon their clothes are snowed on by flaked pastry and scattered nuts, their faces are smeared with butter and honey – and they are smiling at each other …

Monday 2nd April

I heard from the telly company.
I'm in the show. For sure.

The TV people will start with three introductory programmes. We'll just make one dish – our favourite – but most of the cooking and the competition will come after. The first episodes will just be 'getting to know you' time. They will introduce me 'to the viewing public'.

The TV people want everything to happen fast. We are to start recording immediately for these introductory programmes and they'll show them the same day. We'll do them once a week. They want the whole thing to happen quickly because it makes it dramatic – Jules says it'll be like it's happening in 'real time'. The interest will build quickly – and then the real competition will start.

They have given me a publicist. And my first job is to talk to the newspapers about the competition, what I hope for from it, and what happened to get me involved in so much 'negative publicity'. The street fight – and the police caution – have to be dealt with. Also the fact that I am 'different'. A foreigner.

'We will deal with the fight incident,' said the publicist, 'and we will turn it around. Just you wait and see.'

I go into their office after school with Angie, the library lady, as my 'appropriate adult'. I am asked to read my answers to those two questions again.

The cameras run. I am asked about the incident in the park and I tell them what happened and about my neighbours and the lollipop man coming round to the flat to tell me that they would support me. I also tell them about the party I had and I show them the photos.

I tell them this will be my first recipe to demonstrate – the pumpkin patties. When they ask about my recipes I tell them the story of my recipe book. I show them the battered book with its sticky stuck-down pages and its bent corners. I tell them about the other people I imagine have used this book and I tell them about the video chats with my mum and my grandmother.

The camera is turned off. Jules shakes my hand.

Then Angie drives me home.

'You did well,' she said and she smiles.

Tuesday 3rd April

I was on the teatime telly news.
I was in the local newspaper.
I was in the national newspapers.
I was in that newspaper – the one that called me

'troublemaker' and all those other awful things.

They seem to have changed their mind about me. I feel like a little parched plant that has suddenly had a lovely long cool soothing shower of water. I feel clean and fresh and full of life and excitement.

'A star is born,' says my bro – with a tinge of bitterness – but he pats my back. He is pleased really.

My dad manages a small smile but his mind is elsewhere.

They wave me off.

I set off for school with a slight spring in my step.

I pass Katie's house. She comes running out waving a bunch of mint.

How much mint does she think I need?

Plus this mint looks a bit limp. As if she has been clutching on to it for some time waiting to see me and pass it over.

Wednesday 4th April

It really is hard to concentrate in lessons now, but everyone seems to understand this somehow – why didn't they understand this before?

Keef's gang has dwindled back to its original number and even they don't seem keen on picking on me.

They didn't come out of that news story very well. The lollipop man popped up on the news with his story of what he had seen of the fight, and some of the neighbours appeared with their views and stories about my family and my party. The lady with the cats was particularly kind – plus she had filmed some of the party on her phone. They stood up for me. It made me smile.

Thursday 5th April

The TV company are in touch all the time now. I have to work on possible menus and send them in. They say *they* will get all the ingredients. They will provide all the pots and pans. I will be able to have everything I need.

They asked a strange thing.

They want to record more of my video calls and discussions of my cooking with my mum and grandmother.

'We won't use it all,' they explained, 'but some footage of your gran and mum passing on their advice to you – from ... where they are ... will be good. It will help the public to get to know you and understand you. We'll discuss it with your dad and your teacher. It could be a great extra touch for the programme – and it might have publicity benefits for your family.'

What do they mean 'publicity benefits'?

Friday 6th April

Sports practice after school. All my team are thrilled and excited and interested in me.

Mr Jones asks me how I feel about 'the fund'.

I have no idea what he is talking about.

Saturday 7th and Sunday 8th April

I understand now. I know what 'the fund' means and what 'publicity benefits' are.

That newspaper – the very one that caused all the trouble for me, that called me names – that one …

Well it has 'changed its tune'.

Now it has decided to back me.

The newspaper has printed the story of how I was 'falsely accused of a violent affray'. (It doesn't mention that it was one of my main accusers.)

It explains to people about all the things I have gone through and all the progress I have made and how my 'dearest wish' is to cook a wonderful meal for my mother and grandmother for my mother's birthday.

I am sure I didn't actually say that bit about my mother's birthday.

It tells the readers that I am working on a perfect menu

to offer to my mum when I see her – if I ever see her it adds (and my heart does that flipping over and landing in my boots trick it does sometimes). It tells everyone how I long to make healthy food and nourishing soups for my sick sister.

I don't think I have ever mentioned soups for my sister.

It has bits of truth in there, but lots of exaggeration. I am flabbergasted, but Miss Noon says that's the way that particular newspaper is.

'They are never one hundred per cent accurate – but at least they are on your side now,' she says.

I feel ... swept along by it ...

Monday 9th April

We went to the studio and I made the first dishes – the pumpkin patties. It was shown this evening. And now ... The fund! It seems that I am not the only one to be swept away by this story. People – newspaper readers – members of the public – have been sending in money to help us. We can see it building up online. Pensioners have been sending in their precious fivers, children have sent their pocket money, rich businessmen have been sending in huge picture-opportunity cheques, the local MP says she is helping with the paperwork and everything that can be done is being done and her party has always supported the refugees. This is not what she said the last time my dad tried to get some action from her. Then it was all 'it's very difficult ... these things take time ... we have to be realistic.'

We don't know if she can change things for us or not, but we hope ...

Joram gets every newspaper he can find. He has a slight look of hope about him now.

My dad looks bewildered – hopeful, worried, anxious, over-excited, ill – all at the same time.

The newspaper calls these the 'rollercoaster days' and for once I think they have got it just right. All these sudden swoops and lifts, these hurtles and hurdles, the fear of falling, the excitement, the terror ... it's all here. I am living a part dream, part nightmare.

I seem to be holding my breath.

'In, out,' I tell my lungs, 'take your time. And Head – stop spinning now, please. Legs, stop shaking. Heart, stop hoping – in case you get broken again.'

Tuesday Wednesday Thursday Friday

The days are going by in a blur.

A blur of excitement. And worry. And hope. And anxiety.

The phone is always **ringing**. The email is always **pinging**. Reporters run after us and ask questions. They followed my brother to his car-washing job – which was supposed to be a secret job. He has been trying to make money. He was saving up.

They followed me to school and somehow they have got a copy of my poem. I think it was pinned to a display wall. Anyway now it is in the newspapers. They asked me about it.

In reply I gave them another poem.

I wrote it specially.

Anyone can be a refugee
All it takes is one day
One nod
One paper that is signed
Or not signed.
One bomb
One crash
Then lives splinter, hopes dash
Pack up your home.
You're alone.
Begin the walk
Step one, two, three
You, too, could be a refugee.

The MP actually came to our flat.
She had her photo taken with us.
She shook my dad's hand.
'We are taking all the necessary steps,' she says.
I wish I could tell her how many steps we have taken.

The steps round our house back in our old country all that time ago – picking up our possessions. The steps out of our by-now dusty city, down the many roads, steps through the heat of the sun, the cold of the night, steps through the dry dry dust, steps through the flooding rain. Many steps to get us where we are.

We have taken all the necessary steps.

Now it looks as if people want to help us. Because I can cook?

Monday 16th April

We are making recordings for the next episode of the show and it is agreed that we will include a call from my mum and my gran to give me advice on my upcoming recipes.

But we have hit a problem.

Sometimes the connections don't work. The phone is unanswered.

This is one of those times.

We don't seem to be able to get through.

This is disappointing. Bitterly, bitterly disappointing – because I wanted to tell Mum the news.

Dad has come into the studio too, with my brother. We wanted to announce that I had made it through to the competition and that there is a fund and support gathering strength. Help is possible.

It's the best news we have ever had and we are bursting to share it with Mum. I have imagined her face breaking out into a beaming smile. I have imagined Leila chuckling and waving. I have imagined Grandmother getting the twinkle back in her eye.

We had planned on telling them tonight. The TV people were keen to record us telling them this – and it is due to be broadcast. But we can't make the phone and film link work.

'Don't worry,' says Jules. 'We can try again in an hour. Give us some time to make the link. Even if we have to do it live, we will do it! Don't worry.'

But I do worry. What has been going on? Why are the connections down again? Has something awful happened to Mum and Gran and Leila?

We sit in a room and wait. I have a glass of cool water with lemon in it. Dad and Joram have tea. There are biscuits. My dad has an odd faraway look in his eyes. Is he giving up? Is he tired? Or is he now making firm plans to take me and Joram back 'home' so that the family can be together again? I want to help Mum, but I am terrified of going back there. It's a nightmare.

* * *

Two hours later, we are all back in the TV studio again.

There's a flurry of panic. The episode is meant to be on the screens soon, and we haven't filmed it yet. Everyone at the TV station is working fanatically to get the film/phone connection to Mum set up.

'There have been some incidents in your home town,' says Jules. 'Heavy shelling is reported. A lot of connections are down but we have good links with TV news teams in the area. They have offered to help. It's a big risk, but ... we're going to film it live.'

And we do.

And there *has* been heavy shelling.

The pictures of the area show a scene of complete devastation.

The news team who are doing this link for us start by showing an overview of the area. We see a children's playground, destroyed. A tattered teddy bear lies among the dust.

Streets have disappeared. Buildings can no longer be identified. They are just heaps of stone and bricks. The air is foggy with dust. All colour has been washed out and replaced by ash grey and grim brown.

The camera is on Mum. She is sitting outside, on the ground, in the near dark. She is staring into the camera. She is clutching Leila, who has her eyes closed. Behind her there is a space where my grandmother ought to be.

Mum wipes her face and rubs her eyes. She looks exhausted.

'There has been a lot of shelling,' she says. 'Our street is gone. And the hospital – most of the hospital has gone now. Your grandmother was there. She was trying to get medicine for Leila. We haven't heard anything from her since the explosions ... There are people digging through the rubble. We've been there. Digging with our bare hands ... but it is dark now.' She trails off. 'Everything is dark ... '

The camera pans back to show my mother sitting with others near the ruins of a building. That building was apparently the hospital. Somewhere in that wasteland of destruction is my grandmother. She may be dead. She may be exploded. She may be trapped under stones trying to breathe.

The news team make this clear to us, then they show us dusty men and some women and even kids digging, digging, digging and calling out to find people.

I lean forward to speak, but the screen goes to black. Our little film is ended.

And there I am, sitting with my dad and my brother

on a cool leather sofa, behind a shiny glass coffee table in a posh studio in a television company while at the same time our mum and our baby sister are sitting on stones in the dark, and my gran is maybe *under* stones in the dark hoping for someone to rescue her. Maybe she is wounded. Or maybe she is dead. This all seems too unreal.

The TV people look upset and uncomfortable. They don't seem to know what to say.

They are supposed to be making a cookery programme. This is not what they expected.

Jules clears his throat.

'Listen, mate,' he says to me, 'we are so sorry. We will do whatever can be done. We will try … ' But he trails off too. What actually can we do?

We go home in silence. Deep in our own thoughts, our own worries, our own regrets.

The TV company provides us with a taxi so we go home in some style, and I can't be the only one aware of the difference between our lives here in our new home and our mother's life back in our old country.

It seems so wrong. I feel so guilty. My dad looks stricken. And desperate.

We close the taxi door and walk over a completely safe pavement – no holes, no landmines, no stones about to tumble on us. We go over to our own front door, where our own parcels and post are safely delivered to us every day. Security lights come on. Security! We unlock the door and turn on the light. Electric light just like that. Inside we have heat, we have water, we have a landline telephone that works.

In fact the phone is blinking at us. Its little red light is going on and off, off and on. We have a message.

We press the button. We have more than one message.

We have millions of messages. Well, maybe not millions – but many. Many.

Messages from all sorts of people – ordinary people, friends and neighbours. Newspapers, television news, publicists, magazines, the MP. Everybody has seen our broadcast. Everybody wants to offer sympathy. Or money. Or actual help.

There are people with expertise, people with sniffer dogs, people with equipment for finding people underground, people with planes, people with connections, people with money, people with nothing but some understanding of what we are going through and a wish to offer comfort.

The world seems a little better.

We go to bed knowing that all around the country, all around the world, there are others who are working or talking or sharing or thinking and we are all trying to find my grandmother, save my family – get us back together again.

Tuesday 17th April

The next day dawned. I blinked. Rubbed my eyes. Gathered my thoughts. Tried to grasp what was going on. Maybe I was still asleep. Maybe I was dreaming?

The first thing was the radio. We were on the radio news. They were playing extracts of Mum talking yesterday. Commentators popped up to discuss it. Suddenly the whole country seemed to be aware of my situation – my family's situation – our worry, the war we were involved in, the fact that we were just normal people caught up in a situation we had not asked for or caused. The newsreader read a part of my poem.

> Anyone can be a refugee
> All it takes is one day
> One nod
> One paper that is signed
> Or not signed.
> One bomb ...
> ... You, too, could be a refugee.

Things were happening. Money was being gathered. Calls were being made. Suddenly, we were being called a 'special case'. Action was being taken.

The search for bodies and survivors under the ruins

of the hospital was intensified. Later when I switched the telly on, I saw films of teams, with equipment, digging. They had lights now. They had equipment. They were moving mountains of rocks. They were holding up saved babies, stretchering off rescued patients. There was cheering and clapping.

There was still no sign of Gran.

I had a day of star treatment.
Everywhere I went, eyes were looking at me, hands were shaking my hand, patting my back. I felt confused – pleased that so many people are concerned now, but angry that it has taken them so long to realize what our story means. To understand that we are real people with real lives just like them. And I feel guilty that all the attention is on me and my family when I know for a fact that there are millions of people in the same situation – or worse – than me. Millions of people suffering and being overlooked in my country and in many other countries too.

My head was in a whirl. I felt dizzy with excitement, heavy with dread, elated by hope.

In the end I went to the library to avoid all the attention. Angie let me use the quiet corner and I hunched down over the computer and worked on my diary and my recipes.

I checked in on the news from time to time. I was not the lead story any more. Something else had come along. A politician had made a mistake and commentators were popping up to demand that he be called to explain, be punished, be chased out of office.

I felt strangely weary. I longed to go home, crawl into bed, fall into a deep sleep and wake to find that everything had been sorted.

Eventually the school bell rang and I was first out of the gate, ducking down alleyways, changing my route, sneaking home – avoiding attention as much as I could.

Thursday 19th April

The frenzy has settled a little.

Last night I made a meal. We drew the curtains and we drew together, eating and talking, trying to understand, trying to work out what to do next. Trying to come to terms with this strange stardom we suddenly seem to have.

Jules and his team are in nearly constant contact. Even though they never meant to broadcast that episode live, all their television dreams are coming true. They will have millions of extra viewers. They have a success on their hands and they are determined to exploit it while they can. But I think (hope) that they really do care as well.

They keep an eye on what is happening and keep us up to date. When I tried to explain my mixed-up feelings, Jules helped a bit.

'No need to feel guilty, mate,' he said. 'Be pleased! Sure, all the attention is on you and your family at the moment but the publicity you are getting is helping other people too. Look at the footage of the rescue attempts at the hospital. So much more extra help, so many more extra resources. They may be looking for *your* grandmother, but look at all the other people they are finding. Your one individual situation is easy for people to understand. The plight of a whole country and millions of people is hard to grasp. You've made the situation understandable and now people are trying to help. It's all good.'

He advises us to relax and stay quietly at home as much as possible. He will keep an eye on what is happening and he will 'filter' the information.

This means that he and his team will take over keeping in touch with everyone and let us know what we 'need to know'. He will have all the calls and information diverted to his publicity team. That way we will not be overwhelmed and he says his team will 'manage the story' and make sure we get the most publicity and the most action – and the best chance of success.

I hope that his idea of success is finding my gran and getting all my family back together, but I think at least part of 'success' for him is getting as much interest in his programme as he can.

The interest is already overwhelming – and we haven't even started properly cooking yet.

He tells us to stay at home as much as possible. Leave everything to him and just carry on with our normal life.

Friday 20th April

It's so hard to go to school and have a 'normal' life.

I can hardly remember when my life was normal and cannot imagine it ever being 'normal' again.

But off I go to school. As normal.

I go to lessons. As normal.

I try to take an interest.

And fail.

As normal.

I feel as if I am living on a volcano. I can feel everything heating up and bubbling beneath me.

I know there is going to be an eruption. A big change.

I just hope it is going to be a change for the good.

Still no news about Gran.

All day at school I feel like an alien. Really I feel as if I have just been beamed down to a new planet. Everything is strange. I am living on a narrow edge between dream and nightmare.

I am glad when the day is over and I can scuttle back home.

I open the door. And I reel back as if punched. My living room is packed with people. So many people. So much noise. What?

There's my dad. He looks as if he's had an electric shock. His hair is actually standing on end. And he keeps running his hand through it as if to check this really is his head. He tries to speak to me but he is basically stammering. Making no sense. There's Joram too. Looking dazed and silent. There's Jules and two members of his TV team. One of them has a camera, another has sound equipment. There's the MP. She's looking very important, phone to her ear, darting glances to her assistant who is scribbling notes. And there's a man in a suit who I've never seen before and a woman with a big but rather anxious smile.

And two police officers.

All squashed into our flat.

All heads turn towards me when I come in.

They have been waiting for me.

I think I hear the click of the camera but the sound of my heart banging is the main thing I am aware of.

The MP clears her throat. 'After extensive efforts,' she

says, glancing at the camera, 'I am pleased to tell you that a flight has been arranged ... '

What?

Then someone calls, 'OK, now – let's go!' and everyone seems to be talking at once and I don't hear any more. I think I may have fainted. At any rate I feel blank.

We are bundled out of the door and put into a car and we are driven in a big black posh – and fast – car. We are going to Heathrow airport. Are they going to put me on a plane? Am I being sent back? Is this one of my terrible dreams? Am I asleep?

I have a flashback ...

... FLASHBACK

It's the time when I was hurried out of my old home long ago. I have the same sensations of fear and haste and panic. Panic, panic – like shocks to the brain. My body is shaking, my mind is fizzing. I am finding it difficult to breathe.

What?

I catch a glimpse of myself in the driving mirror. I have the same electric-shocked look as my dad. This is all so fast. So unreal. So impossible.

Jules is asking me questions and telling me things.

I seem to be answering but I am on automatic. I may be making no sense. I can't hear anything except the rush of my own blood and fear. Jules is talking to me. His mouth is opening and closing but the sound is muffled. It is as if I am underwater looking at a distorted world, hearing muffled noises.

I keep hearing the words 'plane', 'airport'. Are they taking us all to the airport and putting us on a plane? Are we all being sent back? I can't catch my brother's eye and there's my dad but he looks vacant. There is a sense of unreality about all this. Surely I am asleep. This IS another of those nightmares?

We pull up outside the airport. No finding a car park or looking for a parking space for us. We drive right up to the entrance and there are crowds of people surging all around us. Police open the door for us. There are words but I don't recognize them. Maybe it is not English. Maybe my feet are not on the ground.

Through the doors we go into the airport. Heads turn, eyes stare, cameras flash. Someone waves and shouts my name. There are so many police. They form a line on either side of me. I am marching between them, but this is not my choice. It is as if I am on a wave or in a hurricane – I have to go along. Am I going to be swept out of this country? Is this it?

Then we are at a gate. There is a closed door in front of me.

Jules and his team and other cameras are jostling us.

Flashes, shouts, waves.

... FLASHBACK

Explosions, flashes, shouts, arms waving, jostling, running and the heart banging, banging ...

The doors swing open. I gasp. Maybe I scream.
For there is my mother. My mother.
She is clutching Leila tightly and she is smiling so broadly I think her whole face is a smile.

I start to run and then I see the wheelchair. Behind her an airport person is wheeling a wheelchair – and in the wheelchair sits my grandmother, tired-looking but smiling. She waves. We all run towards each other. Around us cameras whirr and flash and people shout but all I see is my family.

My whole family together again.
Safe.

Further reading and information

If this book has inspired you to find out more about the experiences of refugees – either by reading stories or non-fiction – there is some information below and some 'Further reading' suggestions on the next few pages.

What does it mean if someone is a refugee?
A refugee:
- is outside their country
- had to leave their country because they were no longer safe, due to conflict, political instability or other reasons.

There are many different reasons why people might not feel safe somewhere. Like Adam's family in this story, many people become refugees to escape conflict in their country. It can be very hard for people to leave a country that is at war in a safe and legal way. People may not be allowed to leave, or it might be very difficult – for example, because the airport has been destroyed.

What does it mean to 'seek asylum'?
When people arrive in a new country they may seek asylum which means that they ask the government of the new country to recognize that they are refugees and allow them to live there. This can take a long time and be difficult because each country has rules about asylum.

Human Rights

After World War Two, the Universal Declaration of Human Rights was drawn up in 1948 to help keep people safe and encourage tolerance and peace between nations. One of the things it says is:

'Everyone has the right to seek and to enjoy in other countries asylum from persecution.'

> What can you do in your school to help encourage an atmosphere that is **safe**, **equal** and **tolerant** for everyone?

Further reading

Here are some other books that you might find interesting.

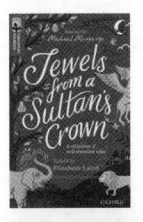

Jewels from a Sultan's Crown
Elizabeth Laird
A collection of wise, funny and inspiring folk tales from all around the world.

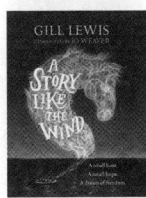

A Story Like the Wind
Gill Lewis
A group of refugees on a boat share stories – dreaming of home, safety and freedom.

If you love cooking, like Adam, you may enjoy reading this book.

Spice Story
Dhruv Baker
Discover the history behind six of the most useful spices, then put them to good use by cooking some delicious recipes.